D0435285

TecnArt
LIVRARIA E PAPELARIA
GALLERIA SHOPPING   TEL (019) 207.3310
R.BARRETO LEME   1210   TEL (019) 232.0422

BRAZIL

DISAL S.A.

Text by
Alberto Taliani

Graphic design
Anna Galliani

Map
Arabella Lazzarin

Translation
Antony Shugaar

Contents

1 This mulatto woman is one of the rainha da festa in the carnival celebrations of Rio de Janeiro. The spectacular costume, the graceful bearing, and even the physical stamina required (the shows last hours and hours, and involve singing and dancing) are indicative of the time and effort that the various groups of the "samba schools" lavish on the preparation of the parades at the so-called Sambodrome. This involve twelve months of very hard work, with rehearsals nearly every day, and tough competition among the loveliest girls, who all want to appear: the carnival is also a form of festival of beauty.

2-3 The unmistakable silhouette of the Pão de Açúcar, or Sugarloaf, which extends toward the bay of Guanabara, is an emblem of Rio de Janeiro: this spur of dark granite rock, some 1,300 feet tall, offers a spectacular view over the city. It seems to shelter the beach that lies before the neighbourhood of Botafogo from the great Atlantic rollers.

4-5 During the rainy season, the Río Negro, which flows into the Río Solimões on a line with Manaus, forming the Amazon river, and the many other rivers in the Amazon basin (there are no fewer than eleven hundred), overflow into the surrounding forest, submerging many square miles.

6-7 The waters of the river Iguaçu, after flowing for over six hundred miles, just before flowing into the river Paraná, plunge suddenly for two hundred and thirty feet, straight down, almost as they have been swallowed up by a cleft in the rocks, into the "Gargantua del Diablo," the Throat of the Devil, one of the most spectacular sections of the waterfall, on the border between Brazil and Argentina; 1.68 miles of frontage of the falls, and the volume of flow, which could fill six Olympic swimming pools a second, make the waterfall one of the most renowned natural phenomena in Brazil. It is a stunning experience to come close to the falls along the walkways or by boat, spattered by sprays of water and deafened by the thundering roar of the liquid flood.

8-9 In the culture of the Yanomami Indians, the little wooden spikes driven through various portions of their faces symbolize the relationship with the spirits of the forest: spirits that control everything but which are also often deceived by fetishes that can cause unhappiness or misfortunes. When this happens, as when illness befalls a tribe member, one must turn to the shaman, or witch doctor of the tribe.

12-13 Ouro Préto, with its spectacular masterpieces of colonial baroque and its art treasures stored up in churches and private mansions, appears as if by magic amongst the green hills.

First published by Edizioni White Star.
Title of the original edition:
Brasile, il verde cuore della Terra.
© World copyright 1995 by Edizioni White Star, Via Candido Sassone 22/24, 13100 Vercelli, Italy.

This edition produced for:
Maytree International Ltd. - UK

Distributed by:
Disal S/A Dist. Assoc. de Livros
R. Vitoria 486/496 - cep 01210-000
Sao Paulo - SP - Brasil

All rights reserved.
No part of this publication may be reproduced, stored in a retrieval system, or transmitted in any form by any means, electronic, mechanical, photocopying or otherwise, without first obtaining written permission of the copyright owner.

ISBN 88-8095-390-7

Printed in Singapore by Tien Wah Press.

ATLANTIC
OCEAN

● FORTALEZA

Á

B U C O OLINDA
        ●
          ● RECIFE
        ● MACEIÓ
SERGIPE

A

● SALVADOR
Todos os Santos Bay

TE

Bandeira

RO

The Brazilian rainforest conceals
beneath the dense and impenetrable
canopy a labyrinth of equatorial plants,
which prosper due to the elevated
humidity of the underbrush, competing
among themselves for the small amount
of light that filters through the leaves.

Introduction

The white hull of the *gaiola* (riverboat) named *Taina* slips through the current of the river that runs through the Great Forest. Along the banks are endless beaches and mangrove prop roots. The sweeping current creates sand banks out of rushing liquid; there are treacherous shallows and immense *igarapés*, the great flood-lakes caused by the terrible high waters of the rainy season, the playland of crocodiles and piranha fish.

The Río Negro, black as ink — as its name suggests — because of the tannin produced by the rotting plants and leaves, runs through the green ocean of the Amazonian forest, in northern Brazil. Just a few dozens miles further on, and one will come to the "metropolis of the rain forest," on an approximate line with Manaus, where the yellowish silty river of another immense river flows into the Río Negro: the Río Solimões, which is the Brazilian name for the Amazon up to this point. This is a liquid universe where the black and the yellow mix lazily, almost reluctantly, amidst whirlpools, wakes, tree trunks, bushes, and dead drifting animals. The so-called *encontro das aguas*, or "meeting of the waters," extends for a good four miles; the banks are separated by the considerable span of eleven miles. And it is here that the Amazon River assumes its name in the full dignity of its renown. Here the horizon is an endless thin green line that veers away from the riverboat when the beds of the two rivers spread out into an unthinkable vastness. It seems never to stop. The *gaiola* chugs along determinedly in the silence, broken only by the sounds of the dense rain forest, or *selva*, the cries of animals that can be heard but not seen, with the dull undertone of the diesel engine. Green and still more green, day after day after day. The immensity and isolation of the Amazon cannot help but be felt by a human being: about two-and-a-half million square miles of jungle.

The Amazon river basin gathers the flow of eleven hundred rivers, and occupies two-fifths of the entire continent of South America. It covers more land than all of western Europe. And the Solimões-Amazon runs from the Peruvian Andes all the way down to the Atlantic Ocean, some four thousand miles through wild and unspoilt nature, an immense watery highway cutting through the rain forest.

Life flows slowly in the small floating world of the riverboat, packed with passengers heading to Manaus, the capital of the Amazon basin.

These passengers boarded a few days earlier at Tapurucuara, at the base of the Serra Parima, which marks the watershed between Brazil and Venezuela. The passengers have stowed their baggage in a huge cage with iron bars, fastened with a massive padlock, in the middle of the lower deck. Then each of the passengers chose a corner on one of the the three passenger decks, on this riverboat with no cabins. People sleep in hammocks. They play cards or checkers, and drink a Brahma or an Antarctica beer. They tell unbelievable stories about prospectors searching for gold or diamonds, swallowed up by the Green Inferno, of immense wealth lost in a few brief hours at the gaming tables, or of duels between *garimpeiros* in search of nuggets. Let it be clear — life is harsh in the Amazon: a daily struggle to survive, which is an adequate description of the lives led by the last dwindling tribes of Indians — just a few more than one hundred thousand individuals, living in one hundred and ninety-eight communities — shouldered aside incessantly by the advance of "civilization," and by the growing exploitation of the natural resources of the land: chiefly veins and lodes of diamonds and gold, as well as bauxite, nickel, and tin. The epic of *caoutchuc*, or rubber, and the *seringuieros*, or rubber-tappers, who harvested the latex of the rubber plantations, ended back in the Thirties. Nowadays the products of the land are hardwoods, livestock, soybean and sugar-cane plantations. There is a struggle to find an absolutely crucial equilibrium between economic needs and the safeguarding of an ecosystem that is essential to the health of the planet.

People work and live in a harsh and unfriendly environment, made up of isolation and great distances that can be covered only by riverboat or by airplane, because during the rainy season the network of dirt roads becomes unusable. Every day, one can happen upon a little adventure. Just the apparently workaday task of supplying an Amazon riverboat with fresh provisions — fish, meat, and fruit — can produce the unexpected. And so it may happen — and it frequently does — that one sees a *gaiola* moored along the river bank, and the passengers and crew going ashore to engage in the risky and perilous capture of a solitary bull, which is slaughtered by brute force and hammerblows, and butchered on the spot. Then the *Taina* puffs and pants her way back onto the river. There is no room for romanticism on the Amazon. It belongs in part to mythology, to legend, and that aspect is continuously fostered, but in reality this area belongs to great travellers, to those who love to discover distant lands. The only radio is in the captain's small cabin, at the helm, next to the wheel. The radio plays a *samba da roda* or a

14-15 *The white costumes of the women of Bahia contrast with their multi-hued of flowers and necklaces. This is the Brazil people of African descent, the children of former slaves, kidnapped from their native continent by the Portuguese in search of workers for plantations and mines. Their traditions live on in the religious festivals: the "Lavagem de Bonfim" is one of the most picturesque and popular events, celebrated by the people of Muritiba, in Salvador da Bahía. And it is in the states of Bahía and Pernambuco that* candomblé *is most popular, a religion that joins saints of the Catholic church with African deities: it is a form of religious syncretism that involves ceremonies that revolve around the mother saint, or* mama dos santos, *the chief figure and the intermediary between deities and the faithful.*

sportscaster announces a soccer game, reminding the traveller that somewhere out there the civilized world still exists, that in Rio de Janeiro or in Salvador da Bahía life goes on, apparently carefree, looking out over the ocean waves, hair ruffled by the sea breezes. For those who live around here, that is how it must seem, far-away, golden, longed after. Dreams. Pictures from the tv screen, telenovelas. The monotony of the river voyage is interrupted by occasional diversions: from time to time one steams past other riverboats chugging upstream, with an exchanging of noisy salutes from the steam whistle. A succession of tawdry floating shacks paraded by, painted light-blue, white, or pink, or other houses up on stilts along the banks. There are the pirogues, or dugouts, of the fishermen. There are pink dolphins that leap out of the water, there is the constant overhead passage of parrots and toucans, and the mournful loitering of the vultures. Every so often one sails past the hulk of a wrecked *gaiola*. They seem like so many phantoms, hindered by the dangling liana vines, the broken dream of a long-ago Fitzcarraldo in search of himself.

After a last meandering bend in the river, the journey comes to an end. Here is Manaus, high on the left bank. Construction yards with towering heaps of lumber, where riverboats are built, floating pontoons where one can fill the tank with gasoline or kerosene. A teeming traffic of small and large boats, loaded down with exotic fruit, bales of manioc, tubs of fish, and *guaraná* roots. They tie up, several boats deep, at the quaint floating marketplace. Further along, freighters, cruiseships, and ships from the Brazilian navy, are all at anchor, while pontoons and barges loaded with freight and supplies are pushed here and there by the tugboats that have steamed up the Amazon from Belém, where the river widens enormously and flows into the Atlantic Ocean: an estuary so huge that here is one of the largest islands on earth, Marajó, nineteen thousand square miles. Manaus is still at the heart of the Amazon: just over a thousand miles from Belém. It too is an island, but awash in the Green Inferno. It was once frontier land, a point of departure for exploration and conquest: for this reason, the Portuguese in 1669 built the fortress of São José da Barra of Río Negro, around which developed the city, which took its name from a tribe of Indians. It sits in a strategic location, at the confluence of the two great streams of Amazon, the Río Solimões and the Río Negro with the spectacular *encontro das aguas*.

Nowadays, Manaus is an immense "backline," the heart of traffic and trade on the Amazon, a warehouse-city where one can find anything, and where everything is shipped off and swallowed up by the forest; an industrial city that has found renewed energy and vigour with the establishment of the free zone and the arrival of multinational electronics manufacturing and Japanese, European, and American light industry. The emblem of the town is the Teatro Amazonas, in neoclassical style, with a yellow, green, and blue cupola, an impressive double colonnade on the façade, Italian marble from Carrara, the stuccos, the tropical hardwoods, and the glitter of the lights. It was inaugurated on 1896 on the orders of the *fazenderos*, the rubber barons, incredibly wealthy owners of plantations who accumulated vast fortunes during the period between the late nineteenth century and the early twentieth century. Everything was brought here by ship from Europe: here Sarah Bernhardt and Enrico Caruso performed, before the "high society" of the rain forest, a high society that wanted all of the glitter and luxury of Paris, London, Berlin, or Lisbon.

In that period, Manaus even had electric lighting, the second city in Brazil to boast this modern convenience, after Rio de Janeiro.

Everything came up the river, following its ocean crossing, at dizzying prices. But who cared? There was plenty of white latex flowing in to feed the new rubber industry. Then came the collapse. The British broke the Brazilian monopoly by smuggling out seeds and transplanting rubber in Ceylon, Malaysia, and Indonesia. The land there was better suited for agriculture and was more productive. That was the beginning of the rubber wars, and the prices plummeted, along with the enormous fortunes of the "rubber barons." Between the Twenties and the Thirties came a long decline; a decline of Manaus, and therefore of the Brazil of nature and adventure. And this is no mere stereotype: just get on one of the many riverboats that cross the *encontro das aguas*, and steam to the opposite shore, beyond the river. One lands amidst a shanty-town and amusement park, where one can gamble and be defrauded rapidly and often. Children play ball amidst vultures loitering with sinister intent. The croupier working the wheel of fortune counts up the winnings with satisfaction; he smiles, perhaps thinking back to the bad old days, when he worked like an ant among thousands of other human ants in the Sierra Pelada, in the state of Pará, men that slave like damned souls in a circle of Dante's "Inferno" to find nuggets of gold. Trucks loaded with merchandise are off-loaded from a raft. Now that the rainy season is over, they can risk running over the road, partly paved and partly dirt, often partly impassable, interrupted by an endless succession of wooden bridges that must be crossed at walking speed, between Manaus and Porto Velho and the Transamazonian Highway, over five hundred miles to the south.

16-17 *The Golden Chapel of Recife, capital of Pernambuco, is a masterpiece of the colonial baroque that flourished here during the seventeenth and eighteenth centuries. Carvings in tropical hardwoods, stuccoes, gilded work, and portraits of a weeping Christ are typical examples of the religious expression of the Portuguese colonists. Among the best known artists, we should mention Francisco Lisboa, known as Aleijadinho, an architect and sculptor, the greatest figure of Portuguese colonial baroque.*

The Amazon is the last frontierland in modern Brazil. From here, one can begin an intriguing "voyage of adventure" to discover the "continent of Brazil." It is a voyage through the alternately cheerful and sorrowful souls of the Brazilians, rocking from *desencanto* and *saudade*, feelings that do not truly contrast, because this is still a single country: one can love it and understand it only by accepting it just as it is — without compromises, and remaining well aware of the fact that reality is a mix of glamour and misery, or immense wealth flaunted in the face of people who are barely surviving from day to day, hoping dully that something will change. And then, only then, the *saudade*, the heart-breaking nostalgia of being in love becomes more powerful than the *desencanto*, depression, and resignation. Isn't it true, after all, that the samba and the bossa-nova provide a perfect and complete interpretation of the soul of Brazil? If so, then many things become clear, because the sad notes are always drowned out by the cheerful notes, full of joie-de-vivre and hope eternal.

Brazil has more than one hundred and fifty million inhabitants, a territory that covers 3,286,475 square miles (making it the fifth-largest country on earth) immense natural resources, but also the largest foreign debt on the planet. Skyscrapers and super-modern areas are bounded by *favelas* clinging to the hillsides, on the outskirts of town and wedged between the luxurious quarters of the big city. That is just how Brazil is. It is diverse in natural terms: from the Amazon rain forests to the wild marshlands of Pantanal and Rondōnia; from the lush greenery of the Mato Grosso to the endless prairies ridden by the gauchos and the herds of the Río Grande do Sul; from the desert lands of the Goiás to the plantations of sugar cane and pineapples in Ceará, in the Nordeste.

The cities, too, are as diverse as can be: Brasilia, a hypermodern metropolis designed by Oscar Niemayer at the command of the president of Brazil, Juscelino Kubitschek, who chose it in 1960 as the capital of the federal republic; São Paulo, a megalopolis that is the industrial and financial locomotive of the nation, and capital of the state in which coffee plantations are concentrated, with over fifteen million inhabitants, appears from the airplane as an endless expanse of skyscrapers, houses, and *favelas*, or shanty-town slums; Rio de Janeiro, sweet and sensual, submerged in greenery and overlooking the bay of Guanabara, "the loveliest on earth," set amidst sugarloaf mountains of black rock and the emerald green of forests and trees, like that of Tijuca, Pão de Açúcar, or Sugarloaf, and Corcovado, or Hunchback; Salvador

18-19 A broad beam and a shallow draft, two or three passenger decks but no cabins: the gaiola *is the typical Brazilian riverboat. In the Amazon basin it is the most common means of transport: riverboats cover the watercourses for thousands of miles; voyages can last for over a week, and one sleeps on deck in a hammock. Often, during these river trips, the* gaiola *will tie up along the banks and the crew will go ashore to find provisions, purchasing food from peasants and fishermen, or hunting in the forest.*

20-21 Sandy inlets, red and black rocks, white lighthouses on promontories — these are all typical features of the Brazilian coastline: the long rollers of the Atlantic, at dawn and at sunset, accompany the fishermen's sailing boats which dot the horizon, daring the open ocean.

22-23 Everyone is taking the spectacular Brazilian sun, lying on the sands of the beach of Leblon, in Rio de Janeiro: with Ipanema and Copacabana this is a daytime meeting spot, a place of fun and excitement. Leblon is Rio's most fashionable beach, with the most desirable crowd. Here, the latest model of swimwear worn by the girls of Rio —the "deltaplane," or "hang-glider" — was introduced, and here, along the beachfront, one will find the most exclusive boutiques.

24-25 At sunrise, on the Barra da Tijuca, there is a time of prayer and invocations. Women wearing the ritual white outfit required by tradition, call on the goddess of the sea, Jemanjá, after tossing flowers and propitiatory gifts into the waters.

da Bahía, colonial and decadent, a splendid city of
art treasures and architecture, the capital of
negritude described so well by Jorge Amado, the
writer who better than any other was able to tell
the "new stories" and contribute to the "new
culture" of the descendants of African slaves.
The result is a "cultural contamination" among
Portuguese, Indians, Africans, new immigrants
from Europe and Japan, and mestizos, that leads
one to reject and ignore the very concept of racism,
although there are still a vast number of social
distinctions and stratifications; still all Brazilians
recognize with pride their unity as a nation: they
salute the flag, they root for the national soccer
team, they dance the samba and celebrate carnival.

All of this can be found in one's voyage of
discovery through Brazil, which has its emblematic
destinations, such as Manaus and the Amazon, but
also Salvador da Bahía (which everyone here calls
Bahía), the old colonial capital, founded by Tomé
de Souza in 1549, looking out over the Atlantic
Ocean. It is the city of Jorge Amado and of
countless classic stories, and a fundamental
stopover on the route into memory, a mingling
between the old and the new: a black face and an
African soul. Here, and in Recife, in Pernambuco,
in fact, the first slaves arrived, imported to work on
the sugar plantations that brought about the
"plantation society" that was so nicely and
thoroughly depicted by Gilberto Freyre in his book
Casa Grande e Senzala, translated into English
under the title, "The Masters and the Slaves."
It is a tough city, difficult to live in, where even the
samba has none of the gentle carioca rhythms of
the sambas of Rio de Janeiro; here the samba is
spare, tough, and syncopated. Bahía is one of the
liveliest and unpredictable of cities. The lower city
is concentrated around the old port, and from
there spread out the boardwalks and beaches along
the waterfront. In the port, near the Mercato
Modelo, the two-masted schooners weigh anchor,
taking boatloads of tourists to discover the tropical
islands of the immense Bahía de Todos os Santos,
slipping past the round mole of Fort Marcelo.
One can take the Elevador Lacerda, an elevator
that rises some 236 feet, and get a view of the
colonial city and the quarter of Pelourinho, around
the Terreiro de Jesus and the Anchieta: churches,
convents, and the palaces of nobility. From the
church of San Francesco al Carmo, to the
Cathedral, to the church of San Domingo: this is a
triumph of Portuguese colonial baroque from the
seventeenth and eighteenth centuries, a spectacle
within the spectacle.

But the true "secret" of Bahía is another, and it
can be found in the poorer quarters, in Rio
Vermelho, on the sea, where they celebrate the

feast of Jemanjá, the black goddess of the sea, or
the cult of Xangó, the god of thunder, or Olorum,
the supreme deity. These are the gods and
goddesses of *candomblé*, the religion of African
origin that led to a fetish cult combining African,
Indian, and Roman Catholic elements, accepted by
the church, so that each deity represents both tribal
tradition and a Catholic saint. *Candomblé* survives
by night in the *favelas*, in popular places of worship
known as *terreiros dos santos*. The deities, through
the person of the *mama dos santos* occupy the
bodies of the faithful, who fall into trances after
hours and hours of dancing to the monodic beat of
ancient instruments of African origin. And Africa
survives in the *capoeira*, the spectacular fighting
dance; in the cooking, with *moqueca*, a dish made
of fish and palm oil *(dende)*, and *vatapá*, made up
of shrimp, bread, fish, coconut, and coconut milk.
Even among these ancient streets and squares,
eroded and marked by the passage of time, golden
in the dawn, while the fishermen haul in their
sailboats while singing songs of praise to Jemanjá,
one finds the soul of Brazil. Just as at Olinda, a
small colonial jewel, set on the hill that overlooks
Recife, or at Ouro Petro, another jewel from the
colonial era.

There is not a place, a city, or a solitary sandy
inlet in the direction of Macejó or Fortaleza, on the
coast of the Nordeste, that does not contain a
surprise or a discovery for the wayfarer. And another
unending surprise can be found in the Brazil of
music and cheerfulness, of the carnival. "Tall and
tan and young and lovely, the girl from Ipanema
goes walking, and when she passes, each one she
passes, goes ah..." — thus goes the myth created by
Vinicius de Moraes, which still survives and
prospers. Indeed, the girl from Ipanema of the
famous song, and the bossa-nova itself, the rhythm
of the school of tropical music of the Fifties, with
such maestros as Vinicius, Jobim, Joao Gilberto
"remain" the emblem and the soul of Rio de
Janeiro after all these years. The city feeds on
samba, bossa-nova, and carnival. They survive and
outlast all fashions, trends, and crazes, and there
have been attempts to define Rio as a "city in
music." There couldn't have been a more perfect
compliment than this, for the *cariocas*.

Is Rio not a *meravilhosa* city? The spectacle of
the bay of Guanabara and its islands, which can be
admired from the Corcovado, at the foot of Christ
the Saviour, and the Sugarloaf, is it perhaps not
unrivalled on earth? And Copacabana, Ipanema,
and Leblon — are they not golden beaches
frequented by *garotas*, the loveliest girls on the
planet? Here, once again, is another sampler of
Brazil's "magic." Rio and its love of life, the long
nights, the five craziest days in the world between

the Sambodromo and Avenida Atlantica, where the *grupos* of the carnival pass by in review.

And perhaps this is the image that everyone wishes to see of Rio and Brazil. Things are not that simple and carefree, however. All one need do is to explore the nineteenth-century section of town or the quartier of the Sahara to discover a different dimension of the city, more relaxed and less glittering. Still, one has to wonder why, when one emerges from one's hotel early in the morning, when the streets are still empty, there is an insistent little air of samba, played by a man on his way to work, on a Coca-Cola bottle with a spoon.

The man has walked down from a *favela* perched precariously on the hill that overlooks Barra da Tijuca, or else from Botafogo or from Flamengo, perhaps. Still, nothing can take away the man's love of life, something like the taste of a glass of *caipirinha*, the national cocktail, sampled at a table in the bar where Vinicius de Moraes composed the *Girl from Ipanema*. He was seduced by the beauty of a girl on the beach. And in the same way, one can be seduced by beauty of Brazil. That is *saudade*.

Ancient and Modern Cities

26 top *This aerial view of the capital of Paraná, Curituba, with a population of over a million and a half, reveals the modern layout of one of the most forward-looking and well-planned cities in Brazil; nonetheless, the modern constructions enclose an ancient soul. The history of the city features European immigrants, as is shown by the historical area of Lagoa da Ordem Santa Felicidade, where there are many quaint Italian restaurants.*

26 bottom *The market of Ver-o-Peso is one of the most picturesque corners of old Belém, capital of Pará and the strategic port at the mouth of the "river-sea," the Amazon. The colonial architecture of the Cidade Velha is distinctive and remarkable; it partly dates from the colonization of the hinterland and the Amazon basin. The city's wealth was derived from farming and exploitation of the land. Cacao, vanilla, cassia, and cinnamon: all the trade was based on what the Indians were able to harvest, and as the tribes were killed off by disease and privations, the period of Belém's decadence began.*

27 *The dark granite* morros, *the tallest of which is the Sugarloaf, or Pão de Açucar, mark off the northern boundary of the beach of Copacabana, the historic stomping gound of the cariocas and the tourists who crowd the great hotels that line the Avenida Atlantica. Copacabana, which is three miles in length, continues to attract cariocas and tourists, despite competition from Ipanema and Leblon. Copacabana is especially popular in the evening, when the strolling vendors create little marketplaces where they sell handicrafts, paintings and clothing, near the hotels.*

Brasilia, utopia attained

28-29 *The political and administrative heart of Brazil is here, in Brasilia, federal capital since 1960. From above, the city is shaped like an airplane, whose cockpit is represented by the sector of the ministeries, by the Plaza of the Three Powers, with the Palacio do Planalto, or presidential residence, the Palacio do Congresso, and the Palacio da Justiçia. The city, built in just three years around an immense man-made lake, created to make the climate less arid, was designed by the urban planner Lucio Costa, the architect Oscar Niemeyer, and the landscape architect Burle Marx. Exceedingly modern, and planned for the use of automobiles and government officials, but not for pedestrians, Brasilia is a success in aesthetic terms, but not in pratical living (a slight problem for the million-plus inhabitants), though it did solve the problem of providing Brazil with a geographically centralized and forward-looking capital, in step with the "dream" of Brazil in the twenty-first century.*

30 *The futuristic corona of cement and glass of the Cathedral is considered to be the masterpiece of Oscar Niemeyer. The interior has a single circular aisle with an altar in the middle, and is set at a slightly lower level than the street outside. The natural lighting is entrancing: sunlight filters through tinted glass panels that soar skywards.*

31 top *Modern architecture dominates the building that houses the National Congress: two slender twin "towers" rise over the main structure, while two half cupolas soften the harsh parallelepiped shapes. Like all of the public buildings in Brasilia, this one is surrounded by many small lakes.*

31 bottom *The Panteão Tancredo Neves, with its eternal flame, is dedicated to the president who defeated the military regime, and to all those who struggled for freedom and democracy in Brazil.*

São Paulo, skyscrapers and high finance

32-33 *São Paulo is the immense capital of the state with the same name, known primarily for its huge coffee plantations; the city is an immense industrial megalopolis, the locomotive of the Brazilian economy, a daunting expanse of skyscrapers that march off into the distance until they are lost to sight. In order to have some idea of the city's mammoth dimensions, one must look at it from an airplane as it lands. A population of more than ten million, 50 per cent of the nation's industry: even though it is a capital of business and manufacturing, São Paulo also has a lively nightlife which revolves around Rua 13 de Maio, Bixiga; traffic is as intense by night as it is by day, including the traffic jams. But São Paulo is also a city of culture, and it possesses some of the most important collections of western art in all of Latin America, in the Museu de Arte.*

33 *The parks, like that of Ibirapuera (bottom) or the handsome gardens of the Government Palace (top), are meeting places for the Paulistas, oases of greenery amidst the cement of the skyscrapers. The park of Ibirapuera is the site of the Museum of Contemporary Art, the Museum of Modern Art, and the Museum of Folklore; near the lake, one will also find the Planetarium and the Japanese Pavilion.*

Rio de Janeiro, cidade meravilhosa...

34   *The beach of Ipanema, the wealthiest and the "youngest" area of Rio, where one can watch the* garotas *— the loveliest young women — was made famous throughout the world by the singer Vinicius de Moraes. Ipanema is an Indian name that means "bad waters": in fact, the ocean breakers often hit the beach so hard and so fiercely that only the local boys brave them with their surfboards, showing off spectacularly in the face of danger.*

34-35   *The immense statue of Christ the Saviour, atop the Corcovado, seems to embrace Rio de Janeiro and the bay of Guanabara. The statue stands at an elevation of 2,325 feet, is a hundred feet tall, and weighs more than a thousand tons. The summit of the Corcovado can be reached by a little rack-railway, which climbs through the dense tangle of the Tijuca, the world's largest natural forest inside a city.*

36-37   *The thousands of lights of Rio glitter in the hot inviting night, and the Sugarloaf is like a lighthouse, illuminating the carioca nights. Alongside the most famous spots and tourist attractions, there are others, less renowned, in which Brazilian singers and musicians perform repertories of samba, bossanova, and jazz: they are in the area of the Sahara, in the old part of town, and in the poorer areas, such as Flamengo.*

34

Recife,
Venice of Brazil

38 Recife, which has also been nicknamed the "Venice of Brazil" because of the many bridges built over the two rivers that run through the town, takes its name from the recife, or breakwater that protects the long beach of Boa Viagem. Recife is an exciting city in cultural terms as well, and it has a complex and intricate colonial history: for many years it was the true "entrance" for the Portuguese, though it was also occupied by the Dutch for a few decades. In the old part of the city, baroque churches and palaces, with their gilt carvings, coexist side-by-side with the riverfront houses with facades like those of Amsterdam. Particularly worthy of mention is the Fortress das Cinco Pontas, built by the Dutch in the early seventeenth century, and the Cathedral. One should also make a point of touring the nearby Olinda, set on a green little hill overlooking the sea; this town was the first capital of Brazil, and it is a "baroque dream," that has withstood the test of time because it still possesses the distinctive baroque architecture of the period.

39 *The market of Recife is held in the historical section at the middle of town, amid baroque churches and mansions, monuments to the colonial achievements and to the wealth produced by the plantations of sugar cane of Pernambuco. In the seventeenth century, the plantations made Olinda and Recife, as well as Salvador da Bahia, the wealthiest cities in Brazil. The slave trade, too, with the slave ships arriving regularly, was a flourishing source of wealth. Precious manpower in the form of stolen Africans, was indispensable in the cutting and harvesting of the sugar cane.*

The lesser capitals

40-41 *Porto Alegre, capital of Río Grande do Sul, located along the Río Guaiba, is a modern city, with a major university and a marked gift for trade: the port is used in the export of foodstuffs and textiles.*

42 *Sailboats in the marina of Salvador da Bahía, from which cruises set out for the green islands and luxuriant tropical vegetation of the Bahía de Todos os Santos. In the background, one can see the skyscrapers of the modern city, and further down, the old port warehouses where sailing ships once loaded and unloaded freight. The port of Salvador was defended by many forts, the most distinctive of which is the Forte Marcelo, in the middle of the water, with its rounded walls, which Jorge Amado once described as the "bellybutton of Salvador."*

43 top *An aerial view of Belém and its port, which lies on the southern shore of the immense mouth of the Amazon. This is the port of the Amazon basin, for the centuries the entrance for those who wished to explore, conquer, or exploit the Green Inferno. Here one arrives from or one sets out for Manaus, through here passes everything which is manufactured or is dug up in the Amazon basin and in the state of Pará. Facing Belém extends the immense river island of Marajó, created by the two main branches of the river as they flow into the Atlantic Ocean.*

43 bottom *Camboriú, the beach and skyscrapers on the Ilha Catarina, near Florianópolis. The island, which bears part of the city, has a number of lovely beaches, such as Praia Grande, which is still unspoilt and nearly ten miles in length, Praia do Santinho and Barra da Lagoa. Praia Mole and Praia Joaquina are the chosen territory of the surfers, on the other hand. Florianópolis is a modern city, the capital of a southern state that has been home to sizable settlements of German and Italian immigrants, with landscapes and farms that are reminiscent of Europe.*

44-45 *The* gaiolas *dock at Manaus: every day dozens of these riverboats arrive, loaded with tropical fruit, fish, and other goods. This is the picturesque floating marketplace of the Amazon basin, with a lively and poverty-striken commerce carried on near the wooden houses raised on poles, characteristic of Manaus and the Amazon basin. This setting shows how the city lives by the river and through the river, a veritable flowing highway. The trading goes on near the Mercado Municipal, with its art-nouveau architecture, built in cast-iron at the end of the nineteenth century. The construction material was brought by ship from England to Belém, and from there by riverboat up the Amazon, to Manaus.*

46-47 The splendour and the
decadence of a capital city coexist
cheek-by-jowl: from Rua da Passo one
can see the church of the Holy
Sacrament and the colonial houses of
the Pelourinho, the old part of
Salvador da Bahía as described and
recounted by Jorge Amado in his books.
It was Amerigo Vespucci who named
this immense inlet the Bahía de Todos
os Santos: the date was the first of
November, 1501, All Saints' Day.
Then, in 1549, Tomé de Souza
founded the city on the highest cliff
overlooking the bay. Until 1736,
Salvador de Bahía was the governor's
residence, the second-largest city in the
Portuguese empire, following only
Lisbon; the urban area developed on
two levels, the Cidade Baixa around
the waterfront, with the commercial
and popular sectors, and the Cidade
Alta, aristocratic and wealthy,
abounding in baroque treasures, as it
has remained until the modern day.
The two towns are linked by the
Elevador Lacerda, an elevator some
two hundred and eighty feet tall, built
in 1868. Sugar cane, tobacco, gold,
diamonds, silver, and livestock all
contributed to the rivers of cash that
enriched the city and filled the coffers
of the empire. In 1538 the first slaves
arrived, and later more came, till half
the population was black. For this
reason too, the Pelourinho is the
emblem of the Cidade Alta: in the
main square, whose name means
"pole," slaves were sold or punished.
The Terreiro de Jesus, overlooked by the
Cathedral and other important
churches, is instead the "sacred
square," or place of faith.

47 São Luis do Maranhão is the only
city in Brazil founded by the French,
who landed on the coast of the Nordeste
in 1612. Three years later, the
Portuguese expelled them, and the city
became a major trading port, first for
sugar and later for cotton. The old city
has a remarkable layout, with long
rows of houses with painted façades,
clambering up the slopes of the
highlands: the Commercial District is
one of the most distinctive corners,
near the rounded Mercado Grande, a
place where one can explore and find
treasures, among the handicrafts and
the delights of the Creole cuisine.
Here, authentic folklore survives,
emerging in the festival of the Bumba-
meu-boi, with the celebrants who wear
traditional costumes and masks.

48 Children in costume take part in the Lavagem de Bomfim, a traditional festival of Salvador da Bahía. As far as festivals go, for that matter, the city is lavishly endowed. Carnival, for starters, is different here from that in Rio, because there are no musical groups playing sambas, but rather, the trio eléctrico, made up of three musicians. Then there is the procession dedicated to the Senhor Bom Jesus dos Navegantes, held on the eve of the New Year. The festival of Bomfim, on the other hand, is linked to the cult of candomblé and the god Oxalá, while the festival of Jemanjá is dedicated to the sea goddess of that name.

48-49 Two girls wearing traditional costumes stop before a church of Pelourinho in Salvador da Bahía. This scene seems to emerge from the stories set in Bahía by Jorge Amado.

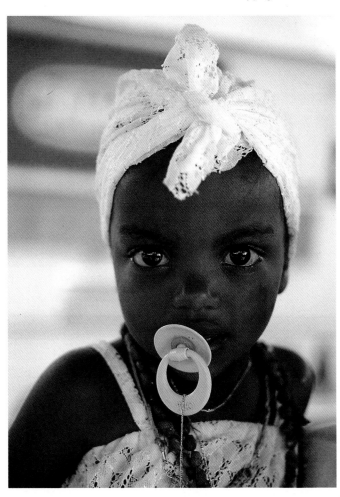

50-51 The ancient splendor offers mute testimony to the important role that Serro, midway between Rio de Janeiro and Belo Horizonte, once played, first during the gold rush, and later during the diamond rush. From the sixteenth to the nineteenth centuries, two-thirds of the gold sent to Europe came from the mines of Brazil.

An Incredible
Melting Pot of Peoples

52 top *The Kamaiura Indians, a small tribe that lives along the Rio Xim, shown locked in a ritual duel, struggling to express power and supremacy in their social hierarchy. For the Indians, the role of warriors and hunters is traditionally very important. Men have the responsibility for procuring food by hunting and fishing, but also by planting fields of manioc, corn, and rice.*

52 bottom *In Brasilia, automobiles and pedestrians never meet: each follow roads of their own. Even the stoplights have been eliminated wherever possible. But if one has no automobile, it is difficult to get from place to place, because the distances are huge and the public transportation is not very efficient. This is not exactly a city "built to the measure of man." Whoever can afford to take a plane back to Rio does so on the weekends, and many government clerks and officials are "air-commuters"; some would like to return the capital to Rio de Janeiro.*

53 *The grupos of the schools of samba parade through the streets of Rio de Janeiro. Costumes, music, and elaborate designs mark the passage through the Sambodrome; on either side of the street are bleachers and boxes from which celebrities and officials watch the parade. No one wants to miss the show, and to have a box at the Sambodrome is an exceedingly prestigious distinction: the sixteen most important and famous groups parade here, vying for victory. The jury judges the schools according to the musical motif selected, the ability of the percussionists, the songs, the quality of dancing, the costumes, and the choreography that accompanies the parade.*

Beauties on the beach

54 *The beaches of Rio de Janeiro are a meeting point between the local youth culture and the tourists: Copacabana, Ipanema, Leblon, and Barra da Tijuca are always teeming with sunworshippers, in part because there is no fee to use the beach, which is often crisscrossed by strolling vendors who proffer tropical fruit, beverages, ice cream, and delicious spits of roasted shrimp.*

55 *The beaches teem with* garotas, *the lovely young mulatto or white women who dedicate their lives to caring for their bodies, helping Rio de Janeiro to deserve its nickname of* cidade meravilhosa; *many of these young women also belong to the so-called schools of samba, and participate in the processions of carnival. Along the beaches, they celebrate the rites of the body beautiful: in the early morning, the beaches are already crowded with young men and women jogging and*

working out along the ocean, all to the rhythm of the samba, of course. The perennial tanning and the beach-front fashion shows are just part of daily life in Rio de Janeiro, as is nightlife and the incessant whirl of fun. The garotas, *as well as carnival, are emblems of Brazil.*

56-57 *The Avenida Atlantica in Ipanema, the most chic part of Rio. The rays of the setting sun light up the sand, the palms, and the houses with highlights of red and gold. The beach has emptied out by this point, and people go home, only to emerge again a few hours later, around midnight. The day has certainly not ended: the discotheques, the bars that pulse to the bossa-nova, and the fashionable nightclubs all invite the visitor to have fun until dawn.*

Divas of the Carnival

58-59 *Scenes of the Carioca carnival, bursting with life and vitality, frenzied and increasingly fanciful, year after year. The Diva is always the focus of attention: usually, the Diva is the loveliest young mulatto woman, a flawless samba dancer. Her costume must capture the attention of the public, and constitutes the pivotal point of the choreography, different every year. Each group parades according to specific rules, and in the street the group is followed step by step by incessant "field producers."*

60 top *The costumes, the make-up, the selection of the materials are all a function of the overall theme that has been chosen for each year's carnival, and are dictated by the imagination and the skill of those who prepare it and who take part. The so-called schools of samba organize lotteries in order to finance the purchase of costumes, while the wealthier citizens may buy a costume for those who cannot afford one. There are many famous designers and dressmakers who work with the "schools" and samba groups. There are old and venerated traditions, such as that of keeping the costume one has worn in a place of reverence in the home.*

60 bottom and 61 *Two of the most famous schools of samba on parade: the "Padre Miguel" and the "União da Ilha." There is no richer, more colourful, or more exciting carnival than that held in Rio de Janeiro. The first popular carnival of the city took place in 1854, and the tradition has been traced back to the great festivals held on the Azores, with a powerful influence from African music and local tribal rhythms. In 1928 the first modern school of samba was founded, the "Deixa Falar." Over time, the number of schools increased, and their activity was strictly codified. They were organized on a voluntary basis, and they are active all year long, since it takes a full year to prepare for the huge, city-wide explosion of frenzy and joy. After the carnival of Rio, the most famous celebrations are those of Recife and Olinda, in Pernambuco, which feature costumes and allegorical masks, with a decided tribal influence.*

Remembering Africa

62-63 *The local folklore expresses itself in the most remarkable manners, with incessant references to the African roots, as can be seen in the costumes of the* Congada de Fifa *and in the anthropomorphic masks of the* Folia da Reis. *These are all distinctive features of modern Brazil, which sinks its roots in the history of European colonization and the Atlantic coast of Africa. The slave ships brought men and women, as well as their cultures, their traditions, their music, and their instruments, all of which reappear in the great festivals of this land. All of this has been amalgamated with Portuguese culture and with the various other cultures of the other European immigrants who came to Brazil in successive waves, seeking fortune. Thus, Brazil has developed a remarkable folklore, of tremendous allure and appeal.*

64-65 *The distinctive anthropomorphic masks of the* Folia da Reis *certainly hearken back to the African origins of much of the population of Brazil.*

The treasures of the Earth

66-67 *Sugar, pineapples, soybeans, coffee, and cotton: these are just a few of the mainstays of the continent-sized country's wealth. Brazil boasts a substantial expanse of intensive farming. This sector of the economy accounts for about a fifth of the gross domestic product, and it provides work for about a third of the workforce. Half of the agricultural products are exported. It is, however, precisely that agricultural production intended for exportation (for example, the coffee and cacao) that monopolizes arable land and resources that could otherwise be used to feed the population of many states, which now suffer as a result. There is a growing number of plantations of sugar cane, bananas, and citrus fruits. In Brazil, the plantation system is solidly entrenched, a result of the colonial history of the country, encouraged by the immense size of the territories: it is estimated that just thirty-two thousand estates of more than twenty-five hundred acres cover three-quarters of the arable land or pasturage.*

68-69 *Livestock grazing in the Pantanal, the region of the* fazendas *where the cattle-herders still ride only on horseback. These ranches are the largest in Latin America: they are found chiefly on the highlands of the interior and in* *the states to the south, thanks to the climate which makes it possible to leave the animals out in the open. Cattle, sheep, horses, mules, and pigs are the wealth of the ranchers here. Much of this production is destined to be exported.*

Ride,
gaucho, ride!

70-71 *Traditions and ways of life shared with the inhabitants of the pampas of Paraguay and Argentina are carried on by the* gauchos *of Río Grande do Sul; these are the territories of the immense* fazendas *and the most productive livestock pasturage. The* gaucho *lives on horseback, and his clothing, his equipment, and his weapons are reminiscent of long-ago times. Here we see a* baiadero *who summons, with his trumpet, the men who must herd the cattle. A number*

of details stand out in the gaucho's *work clothes: the boots of soft leather, the stirrups and spurs made of chased silver, the short knife on the belt that is used to skin animals.*

72-73 *Romantic traditions, dances, and costumes are the heritage of the dreams and legends, the primitive duels, and life lived in the immense and lonely spaces of the south. This is the surprising and perhaps less well known face of Brazil, where the Río Grande do Sul marks an extreme diversity from the rest of the country. The imprint of the* gauchos *is powerful and can be sensed in the cuisine as well, which in certain ways is similar to that of Argentina: here people eat the* churrasco, *fresh beef cooked over an open flame and served on spits that look like swords. Here Portugal and Spain meet and merge in this borderland that has always been a land of encounters, exchanges, and conflict.*

Sails on the Atlantic

74 *The exhausting day of the fisherman is over, and sunset means it is time to go home and lay down the netting. Fish, shellfish, crabs, and crayfish from the brackish lagoons are eaten locally; in some areas they are served to the growing tourist trade as well. Among the palm groves along the beaches, the fish is served fresh in the charming little wooden "barracas."*

75 *On the beaches of Natal, the wind bellies out the sails of the* yagandeiros, *the fishing boats in which fishermen brave the breakers of the Atlantic Ocean, venturing out many miles from the coast. Here we are off the long beaches and dunes of the coastline of the wild Nordeste: the fishermen venture forth in tiny fleets, and even nowadays are so poor that they still use the traditional sailboats. Even today there are not many motor-driven boats or fishing vessels anchored at the little villages along the coast.*

Magic
and religion

76-77 *This photographs captures the
culminating moment of the rites of*
macumba *of African origin: a woman
falls into a trance, possessed by the spirit
of Xango. The Afro-Brazilian rituals
are deeply rooted, and have served as a
sort of social ligament for peoples of
African origins here.* Macumba *is
practiced in a number of different
variants, the most distinctive of which
is the* candomblé *of Bahía. These are
forms of religious syncretism tolerated
by the Catholic church (Brazil is the
most populous Catholic nation on
earth). Alongside the magical rituals
and more orthodox Catholicism, other
religions survive, imported by the many
ethnic groups that immigrated,
beginning in colonial times (Germans,
Dutch, and Jews) or during the more
recent periods of immigration
(Japanese): Protestantesim, Judaism,
Shintoism, and Buddhism.*

Civilization advances

78-79 *The roar and shriek of chainsaws accompanies the felling of trees in the Amazonian forest, used as hardwoods and in the cutting of roads to connect the inland regions with the coastal towns. The destruction of the natural heritage is often reckless and indiscriminate, and can cause incalculable damage to the world's ecosystem. Unbridled deforestation is continuing at unheard of rates, leaving an arid landscape where only brush and scrub will grow for many years to come.*

79 *A new road is being cut: trees fall one after another, the red earth is stripped bare, and trucks roar eerily through the silence of the forest. Work continues to link other highways to the Transamazon, landing strips are cut for airports, and farming settlements are opened along the roads that the jungle attempts continually to win back from humanity. The race for exploitation becomes increasingly feverish, even though there are efforts to find an equilibrium — almost impossible to achieve — between economic considerations and the protection of the ecosystem. This is the most difficult challenge facing modern Brazil.*

Slaves to the goldmine

80-81 *Like souls in a circle of Dante's "Inferno," men swarm through the strip mines where gold is excavated in the Serra Pelada. This is the gold rush, the dream of wealth that for many (far too many) garimpeiros, or gold-diggers, will remain only a dream. The effort is brutal and exhausting, the heavy bags of gold-ore must be carried on straining backs up the steep ladders. Often* landslides bury many men alive. *The life of the garimpeiros is a harsh one. The villages are made up of tents and shacks, all the necessities of life are sold at astronomical prices, and the hastily improvised casinos do land-office business. Still, the idea of getting rich quick draws ever more new adventurers, willing to risk all, even to kill for gold.*

82-83 *The gold-diggers, or garimpeiros, are often men with nothing to lose, as is the case with peasants who have lost work and land: many of them come from Bolivia, Peru, and Colombia. The strip-mines of the Serra Pelada produce dwindling supplies of gold, and many nugget-hunters have moved elsewhere, chiefly to the Amazon basin, pushing back still more Indians. They even hunt for gold underwater, on the riverbeds, with wetsuits, airtanks, and respirators. Another mine like that of the Serra Pelada lies at Cotia: here too the earth, which is sifted for nuggets by panning and filtering, is carried by human bearers; the shantytowns are veritable frontier cities where scores are often settled with pistols and knives.*

Back to the prehistoric past

84 left *In canoes hollowed out with flame, the men of the Yanomami tribe hunt and fish with poison-tipped spears and darts. Hunting and fishing, along with rudimentary farming, are the essential resources of the Indian tribes, many of which are in perpetual flight before the hostile advancing face of "civilization," as it marches though their lands.*

84 right *Women and children chat in the water, in a sort of rite of purification linked to these ablutions which reconfirm the exceedingly close ties between this tribe and the nature that surrounds them. Nature is never considered to be a hostile presence, but rather a source of life and well-being.*

85 top *A Yanomami man smokes through his nose, using a thin reed. The typical Indian is now in regular contact with Western civilization, as is indicated by the shorts this man is wearing, certainly not part of the traditional dress.*

85 bottom *A circular village in the forest, cleared by fire: this is one of the distinctive Yanomami* shapono *in the upper Orinoco basin. The structure is typical of Amazonian settlements, made of wood, plaited leaves, and liana vines. The circular structure also serves a protective purpose, and is indicative of the presence of a tribal group that is accustomed to moving frequently through unfamiliar territories.*

86 *An Aukke Kayapo woman and child display their bodies, painted with the tribal designs. Among these Indians, the woman has the task of preparing food and obtaining a supply of drinking water. The relationship with* *children is very close, and becomes increasingly important as their numbers dwindle: the uprooting of tribes, diseases, and a rejection of encroaching civilization all lead to drastic reductions in fertility.*

87 *A young warrior of the Kayapo tribe boasts the decorations and ornaments that indicate his prestigious social standing. The warriors of this tribe have always been considered particularly fierce and warlike, always ready to defend their territory; this has been true in recent times as well, though the tribes have generally become less belligerent over the last few decades, as they have become resigned to the incessant onslaught of modern culture. A decisive factor in the survival of the Indians has been the assistance and guidance of missionaries.*

88 A child wearing a tribal costume participates in a village festival. Today there are about one hundred and twenty thousand Indians, living in about two hundred small communities. Many of these communities still carry on their traditions and ways of life, and in a few cases have (and wish) absolutely no contact with outsiders.

89 Two scenes from tribal life: in the picture (top), a child is undergoing the ritual painting of the body, which marks a rite of passage and the child's new status as an adult in the little jungle society. In the picture below, their bodies painted red, black, and white, the women are preparing to hold a ceremony: everyone takes part, in part because the communities are very small (no more than sixty or so members) and no one fails to participate in the most important moments of tribal life.

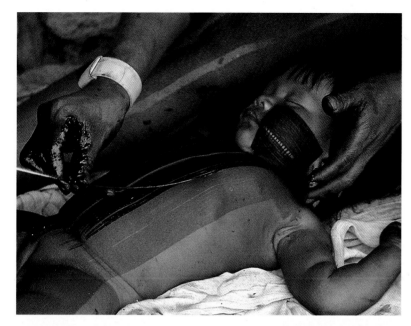

90 left *An Indian of Río Purus poses with a head dress of yellow and red feathers. Here, too, the reference to nature is powerful and direct, as in the feathers of the parrots that inhabit the jungle trees, and which are used here by the young man for ornamental purposes.*

90 right *This picture shows the fearsome Arara hunters, bearded Indians armed with bows and arrows, who have only recently come into contact with European culture. They use primitive bows and long arrows that they shoot with incredible accuracy. The Arara are typical of what have been called the "invisible men" of the jungle, and they have determinedly attempted to avoid contact with the white interlopers.*

91 left *The Matis tribe wear a remarkable "cat-man" mask, which — according to their beliefs — allows them to move easily through the jungle. These people aroused curiosity and fear among the earliest explorers of the Amazon, and the explorers left accounts of them in the journals of their discoveries.*

91 right *The long blow-guns, which are used to shoot deadly darts, their tips dipped in poison, are not only lethal weapons for hunting, but also ancient tools of war. When Europeans first began to explore the rivers of the Amazon basin, they were frequently attacked by the inhabitants armed with bows and blow-guns.*

In order to defend themselves, the Portuguese would cover the bridge of their boats and drape netting over the decks, hoping in this manner to ward off the deadly little arrows.

92-93 *The tribal differences are also expressed though the head dresses of egret plumes and feathers, and by a spike set under the chin. In the communities of the Indians, there are no social classes, and the most important status is reserved for the tribal chieftain and the council of elders. The animals that are hunted and the fish that are caught are all divided up into equal shares, and no stores are set aside for bad times.*

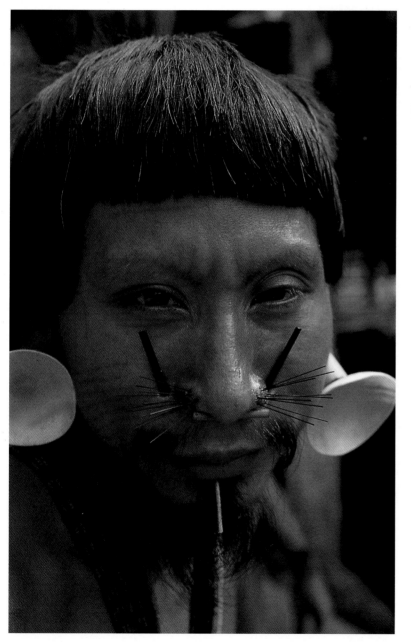

The Last Havens of Nature

94 top *The thousand rivers and streams in northern Brazil crisscross the Amazon basin like so many immense liquid highways: tooling along on high-speed motorboats, one can reach the* igapó *amid leaping pink dolphins and beneath flights of toucans and parrots. Manaus is not far away, but the green horizon dominates everything, heightening the sense of isolation.*

94 bottom *Off the beach of the Island of Cobras, little schooners are anchored, awaiting the tourists who wish to cruise through the Bahía de Todos os Santos, at Salvador, and among the green islands of Rio de Janeiro.*

95 *The jaguar is the king of the jungle: shown waiting in ambush here, this big cat was caught by a telephoto lens as it hid behind a large plant.*

98-99 *Flowers break up the greenery of the Atlantic Ocean rain forest, which covers the cordilleras and mountains of the Serra Graciosa in the state of Paraná, between São Paulo and Porto Alegre, in southern Brazil.*

96-97 *The Mono do Pico and the Cacimba do Padre, in the Atlantic Ocean, just off the tropical coastline of the Nordeste, form the archipelago of Fernando de Noronha, a genuine sanctuary of wildlife and nature: the marine park and nature reserve make this a much admired destination for environmentally minded tourists. The elevation of the Pico, the highest point — one thousand and fifty-two feet — on the twenty-one islands that form the archipelago of Fernando de*

Noronha, is also a true geological oddity because it is the tip of a volcano that rises more than fourteen thousand feet from the ocean floor. The islands have lovely, empty beaches and sea beds that are ideal for scuba diving. Dolphins swim in groups through the bay of Correiro da Pedra or in the bay of Golfinhos; from the beach one can also admire passing whales, while sea turtles lay eggs deep in the sand.

100-101 Immense white sand dunes frame the topaz blue of the brackish waters of a little lake; in the distance one can see the ocean. This is a spectacle that one sees over and over in Salvador da Bahía and along the coasts of the Nordeste, toward Fortaleza and Natal: little miracles of nature, often solitary places where no one goes.

102-103 The thin reddish line of the Transamazonian highway seems as if it is about to be swallowed back up by the forest. This highway, which was built in 1973, is of fundamental importance to the economic and social development of the region: with over three thousand miles of road, it links the Amazon basin from east to west.

104-105 During the rainy season, it seems as if the rivers no longer have banks, and that the "green sea" is going to be swallowed up. The spectacular igapó are created, floodings and marshy swamplands that shrink slowly during the humid hot season. These are a fundamental part of the largest river basin in the world, more than 2.3 million square miles.

In the Green Inferno

106-107 *The Amazonian forest appears as a luxuriant expanse even during the dry season: lianas, underbrush — scanty because of the limited light that is able to penetrate through the treetops, or marshes that expand disproportionately following the rains. The trees can grow to heights of one hundred and thirty feet, and, among the dozens of species (at least sixty have been catalogued), the most common are the munguba* (Bombax munguba), *the pau mulato* (Calycophylum spruceanum), *and the capoc* (Ceiba pentandra).

Ambush among the branches

108-109 *The serpents are special inhabitants of the Amazonian underbrush. The Jiboia, or boa constrictor* (right), *swallows its prey whole, while the green boa* (left) *is a champion at camouflage, and can easily be found wrapped around the branches of the trees.*

110-111 *Particularly skilled at camouflage, the snakes here grow to enormous sizes: like the sucuri, the giant anaconda, as long as thirty feet, capable of swallowing animals weighing one hundred and fifty pounds, after crushing them to death.*

112-113 *After the Amazon basin, one of the most interesting naturalistic areas of Brazil is the Pantanal: forests, marshes, and savannahs occupy an area the size of France, between the Mato Grosso and the lowlands of the Chaco. From October to April, the waters of the river Paraguay submerge the Pantanal: this is the period of flowering plants on the trees, when the migratory aquatic birds arrive. From May to September, during the dry season, mammals once again become the lords of the land: from stags to fawns, from foxes to otters, from anteaters to jaguars, from panthers to leopards.*

The kingdom of animals

114 *The tapir is one of the many inhabitants of the forest; a "little relative" of the rhinoceros, it usually feeds near marshes and on riverbanks, where it walks down into the water.*

115 *This picture shows a herd of capybara with their young in the foreground. The capybara is the world's largest rodent, and it can grow to considerable sizes: as long as five feet, and as heavy as one hundred and seventy-five pounds; it has webbed feet and is an excellent swimmer, capable of remaining underwater for as long as ten minutes.*

116-117 *The universe that these animals occupy is made up of trees and bushes: they are the alanatta (left), with long silky hair, that lives in the Pantanal and the Mato Grosso, and the slow and solemn sloth (right), which is also capable of swimming, adapting perfectly to the natural habitat on those rare occasions when it descends from the tree where it hangs, head downward, for long periods of time.*

118 *An anteater hunts for its chosen prey in a tree. This is one of many inhabitants of the Brazilian jungles and forests; the abundance of fauna, which so many are now trying to protect, is a resource for the development of one of the most modern and intelligent forms of travel — ecotourism.*

119 *The otter too is frequently found in the igapó of the Amazon basin and the marshy areas of the Pantanal. These territories have preserved their nature for thousands of years, and the animals have adapted perfectly to the natural conditions, developing noteworthy survival skills through camouflage and refined hunting techniques. Only in this way has the system succeeded in maintaining a perfect equilibrium — until humans succeed in damaging that balance irreparably.*

120-121 *The long and powerful orange-yellow bill (whose function ornithologists have not yet understood) makes the toucan an unmistakable bird, one of the most likable inhabitants of the forest. It often flies together with macaws, cheerful and noisy inhabitants of the "upper reaches" of the jungle, amid the treetops. Among the ornithological rarities there are the harpy eagle, with powerful talons, and the hoazin, a bird that is considered particularly primitive, a direct descendant of the animals of the Oligocene.*

122-123 *A caiman spreads its frightful jaws: always lying in ambush, ready to strike when the victim least expects it, perhaps while slaking its thirst, this animal is the true lord of the rivers and swamps. The Indians are skilful hunters of caimans, and are capable of determining the length of the beast before attacking it. The smaller specimens are caught by night, along the banks, by hand: a spectacular and often very dangerous technique.*

124-125 *In the quieter bodies of water, one can see the elegant, green, rounded floating forms of water lilies, present in all their many varieties, known as* Victoria regia, *which can grow to be over two yards in diameter. One can also see, in the half-light, red and white flowers, such as the heisteria or airplants, a group that includes more than fifteen thousand species of orchids.*

126-127 *White egrets and scarlet ibises with black bills stand in their chosen environment, a pond of still water, where they feed on little fish and crustaceans. These birds are particularly admired for the beauty of their plumage and for the elegance of their flight, which competes with that of the sun-grebe.*

128 *The inquisitive gaze and timid smile of a girl from the Yanomami tribe.*

Photo credits:

Zeka Arauso / N Imagens:
page 54.

Ricardo Azoury / N Imagens:
pages 34 top, 70-71.

Erwin and Peggy Bauer / Bruce Coleman:
page 95.

Nair Benedicto / N Imagens:
Back cover, pages 12-13, 20-21, 33 bottom, 62, 63, 64-65, 72-73.

Richard Coomber / Planet Earth Pictures:
page 115.

S. Cordier / Explorer:
pages 119, 120.

Susan Cunningham:
page 87.

Nicholas De Vore / Bruce Coleman:
page 26 top.

Lou Embo / Overseas:
pages 48-49.

Francisco J. Erize / Bruce Coleman:
page 118.

Andrea and Antonella Ferrari:
pages 11, 121, 122-123, 125 top.

Foschi / Focus Team:
pages 96, 97.

M. Friedel / Grazia Neri:
page 55 right.

Manfred Gottschalk / Apa Photo Agency:
pages 2-3, 6-7, 34-35, 36-37, 102-103.

Jacques Jangoux / Grazia Neri:
Cover.

Hans Gerold Laukel:
pages 106, 117, 126, 127.

Maurizio Leigheb:
pages 8, 9, 31, 46, 47, 52 top, 75 top, 84, 85 bottom, 88, 89, 90, 91, 92-93, 100-101.

Riccardo Malta / N Imagens:
page 94 bottom.

Luiz Claudio Marigo / Bruce Coleman:
pages 4-5, 50-51, 76, 77, 98-99, 104-105, 107, 108, 116, 125 bottom.

Saulo Petean / N Imagens:
page 86.

M. R. Phicton / Bruce Coleman:
pages 110-111.

Jean Charles Pinheira:
pages 1, 14, 15, 16, 17, 18-19, 22-23, 24-25, 26 bottom, 27, 28-29, 32-33, 33 top, 34 bottom, 38, 39, 40-41, 42, 43, 44-45, 48, 52 bottom, 53, 55 left, 56-57, 58, 59, 60, 61, 66, 67, 68-69, 71, 74, 75 bottom, 78, 79, 80, 81, 82-83, 85 top, 94 top, 128.

Eckart Pott / Bruce Coleman:
page 124.

M. Wendler / Overseas:
pages 30, 109, 112-113.

Gunter Ziesler / Bruce Coleman:
page 114.